Appaloosas

and Other Handsome Horses

by
Rae Young

CAPSTONE PRESS
a capstone imprint

Snap Books are published by Capstone Press,
1710 Roe Crest Drive, North Mankato, Minnesota 56003
www.capstonepub.com

Library of Congress Cataloging-in-Publication Data
Young, Rae.
  Drawing Appaloosas and other handsome horses / by Rae Young.
       pages cm. — (Snap. Drawing horses)
  Summary: "Lively text and step-by-step instructions give an introduction to drawing horses"—Provided by publisher.
  ISBN 978-1-4765-4001-6 (library binding)
  ISBN 978-1-4765-6051-9 (eBook PDF)
1. Horses in art—Juvenile literature. 2. Appaloosa horse—Juvenile literature.
3. Drawing—Technique—Juvenile literature. I. Title.
  NC783.8.H65Y682 2014
  743.6'96655—dc23   2013035800

Editorial Credits
Mari Bolte, editor; Lori Bye, designer; Jennifer Walker, production specialist

Photo Credits
All illustrations are by Q2AMedia Services Private Ltd, except for June Brigman, 30-31

Printed in China by Nordica.
1013/CA21301921
092013   007745NORDS14

TABLE OF CONTENTS

Getting Started 4

Tools of the Trade 5

Golden Grayhound 6

Heavyweight In Flight 8

Draft Pull 10

Spanish Spirit 12

On the Trail 14

Sleigh Ride 16

American Pony 20

In the Air 22

Treat Face 24

Splashed in Paint 26

Bonding 28

Spotted Scenery 30

Internet Sites 32

Look For All the Books in This Series 32

Some artists see the world as their canvas. Others see the world as their pasture! If you're a horse lover, grab a pencil and a notebook. Just pick a project and follow the step-by-step instructions. Even if you've never drawn a horse before, the projects in this book will get you started. You'll have everything you need to draw a funny foal or a record-setting racehorse.

Once you've mastered the basics, try giving your art a personal touch. Customize each horse's saddle pad or halter with bright colors and patterns. Add in details like silver conchos or textured leather. Draw accessories such as winter blankets, first-place ribbons, or buckets and brushes. Why not try drawing your friends on a trail ride or galloping across a beach? Don't be afraid to get creative!

TOOLS OF THE TRADE

1. Every artist needs something to draw on. Clean white paper is perfect for creating art. Use a drawing pad or a folder to organize your artwork.

2. Pencils are great for both simple sketches and difficult drawings. Always have one handy!

3. Finish your drawing with color! Colored pencils, markers, or even paints give your equine art detail and realism.

4. Want to add more finishing touches? Try outlining and shading your drawings with artist pens.

5. Don't be afraid of digital art! There are lots of free or inexpensive drawing apps for tablets or smartphones. Apps are a great way to experiment with different tools while on the go.

GOLDEN GRAYHOUND

The Akhal-Teke is a rare horse bred in the desert. This horse is often compared to grayhounds or cheetahs. Their streamlined bodies make them ideal for endurance. They also excel at eventing and dressage. Make sure you capture the Akhal-Teke's lean look in your art.

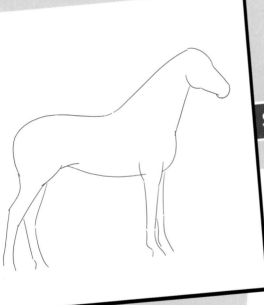

Step 1.

Step 2.

Tip

Have you ever thought of adding silver or gold to your equine art? You're in luck! Akhal-Tekes have hair that has a special core. This core bends light in a way that makes these horses shine. Black horses have a blue or purple sheen. Palominos and buckskins appear gold. Even plain chestnuts and bays can have reddish chrome.

Step 3.

Step 4.

HEAVYWEIGHT IN FLIGHT

Draft horses are good for more than pulling wagons! Many, like this Percheron, are athletic and talented when asked to work under saddle. Their large feet and dense bones absorb impact while jumping. And their willing attitudes make them good riding partners.

Step 1.

Step 2.

Tip

There are many shades of gray to choose when drawing horses. Gray horses can be born any color. Over time, their coats change and lighten. Dapple and rose gray are in-between colors. A mature gray horse is either fleabitten or white gray. This horse is dapple gray.

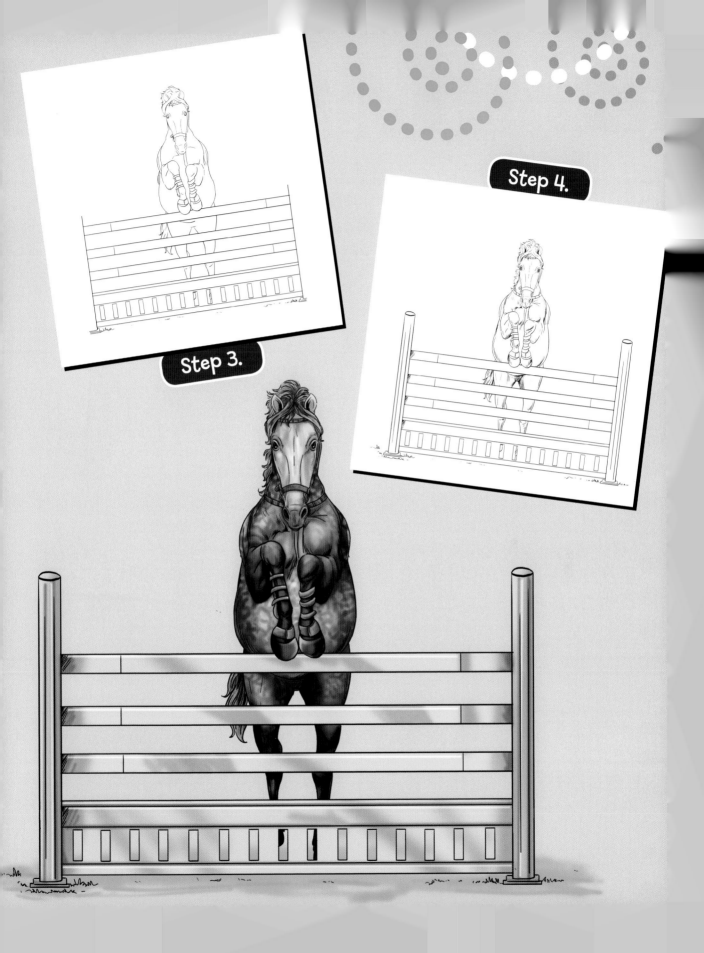

Step 3.

Step 4.

DRAFT PULL

Pulling horses are trained to pull heavy weights over short distances. Like human weight lifters, conditioning a pulling horse takes time. But once fit, a two-horse team of the strongest pullers can move more than 10,000 pounds (4,536 kilograms).

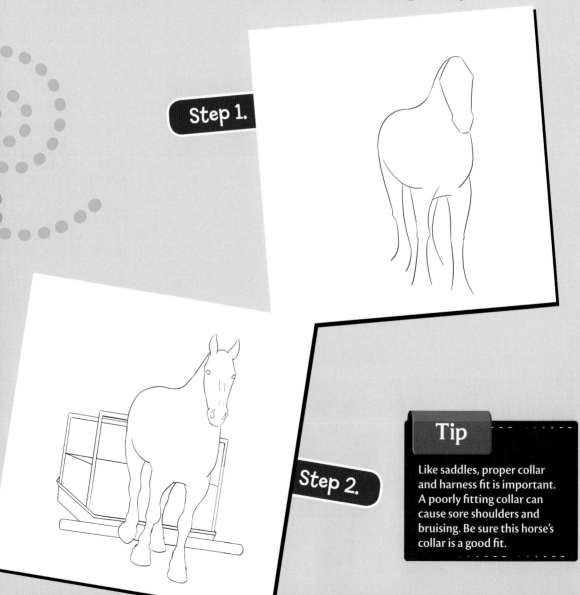

Step 1.

Step 2.

Tip

Like saddles, proper collar and harness fit is important. A poorly fitting collar can cause sore shoulders and bruising. Be sure this horse's collar is a good fit.

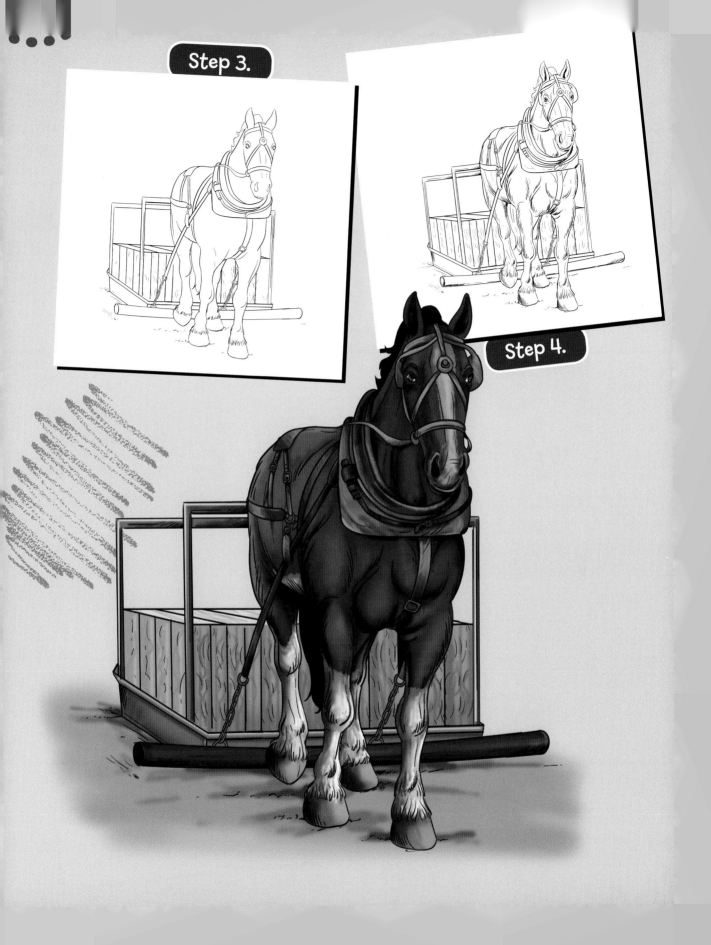

Step 3.

Step 4.

SPANISH SPIRIT

The Andalusian is a Spanish horse that has been around for nearly 25,000 years. It has history as a bullfighter and a warhorse. Today the Andalusian competes in dressage and show jumping, and on the hunter circuit.

Step 1.

Tip

Spanish saddles and bridles are stunning. Add them to your Andalusian for more beauty and drama.

Step 2.

Step 3.

Step 4.

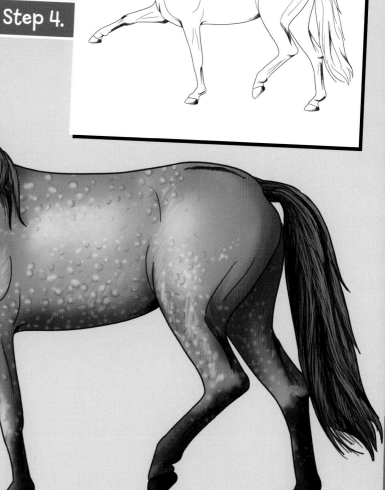

ON THE TRAIL

Competitive trail rides are more than just a stroll through the woods. They usually take place over a 6- to 8-mile (9.7- to 13-kilometer) trail. Horses and riders must navigate a variety of obstacles. They are judged on how well they tackle the obstacles. Obstacles can include crossing water or bridges, opening or closing gates, and stepping over or through vines or logs.

Step 1.

Step 2.

Tip

Use unusual objects to make your drawing more interesting. Poles, tarps, hills, and even fake animals are common competitive trail obstacles.

Step 3.

Step 4.

SLEIGH RIDE

Hackney ponies are smaller versions of hackney horses. Hackney ponies compete in five different classes. They are divided by size, movement, and appearance. Hackney ponies are usually shown in halter or are driven.

Step 1.

Tip

Although hackney ponies are usually driven, they can also be trained to ride. Switch out the sleigh for a saddle!

Step 2.

Step 3.

Step 4.

Step 5.

17

Step 7.

The Pony of the Americas, or POA, is an American breed developed in the 1980s. The first POA was a cross between a Shetland pony and an appaloosa. Today the POA is the perfect breed for families and children. Only children under 18 can show a POA under saddle. So why not add yourself as this pony's rider?

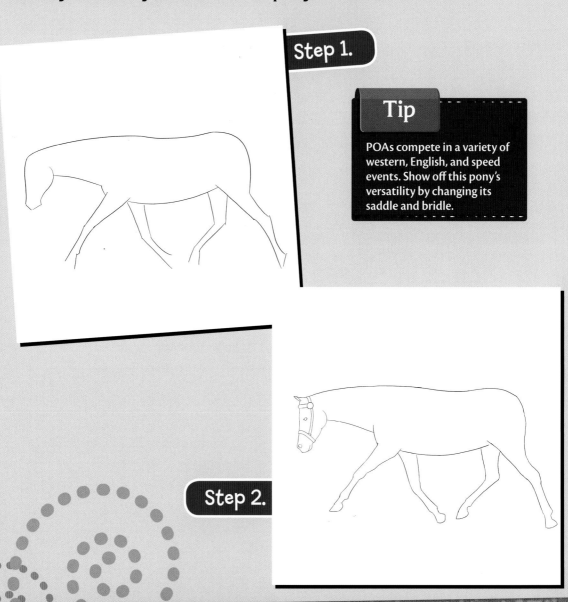

Step 1.

Tip

POAs compete in a variety of western, English, and speed events. Show off this pony's versatility by changing its saddle and bridle.

Step 2.

Step 3.

Step 4.

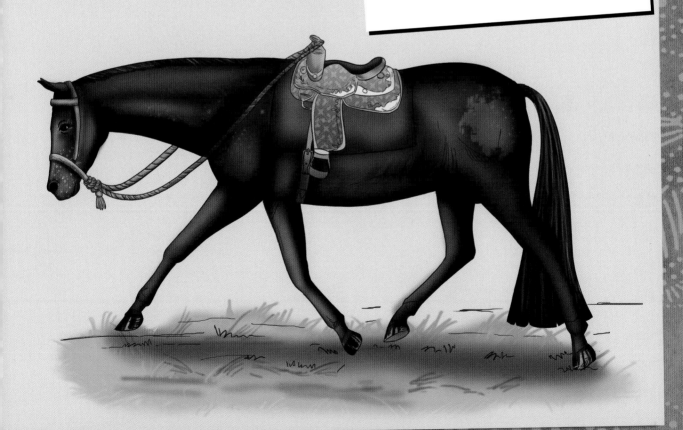

IN THE AIR

Show jumpers try to jump higher, wider, and faster than anyone else. An Olympic jump can be 5.2 feet (1.6 meters) high and 7.2 feet (2.2 m) wide. A water jump can be 14.4 feet (4.4 m) across. That's a lot of ground to cover!

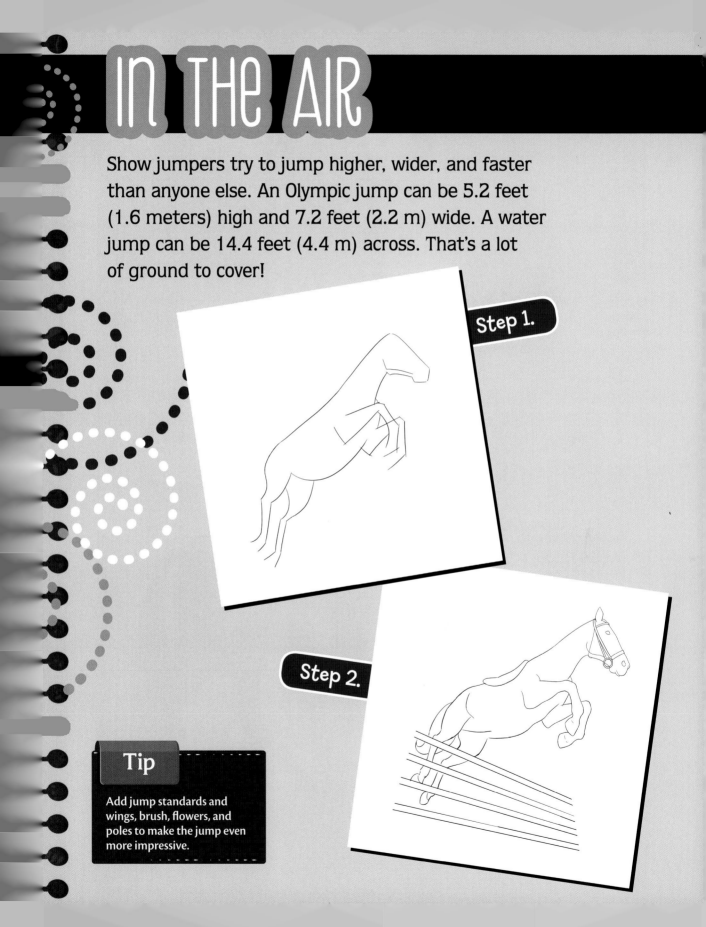

Step 1.

Step 2.

Tip

Add jump standards and wings, brush, flowers, and poles to make the jump even more impressive.

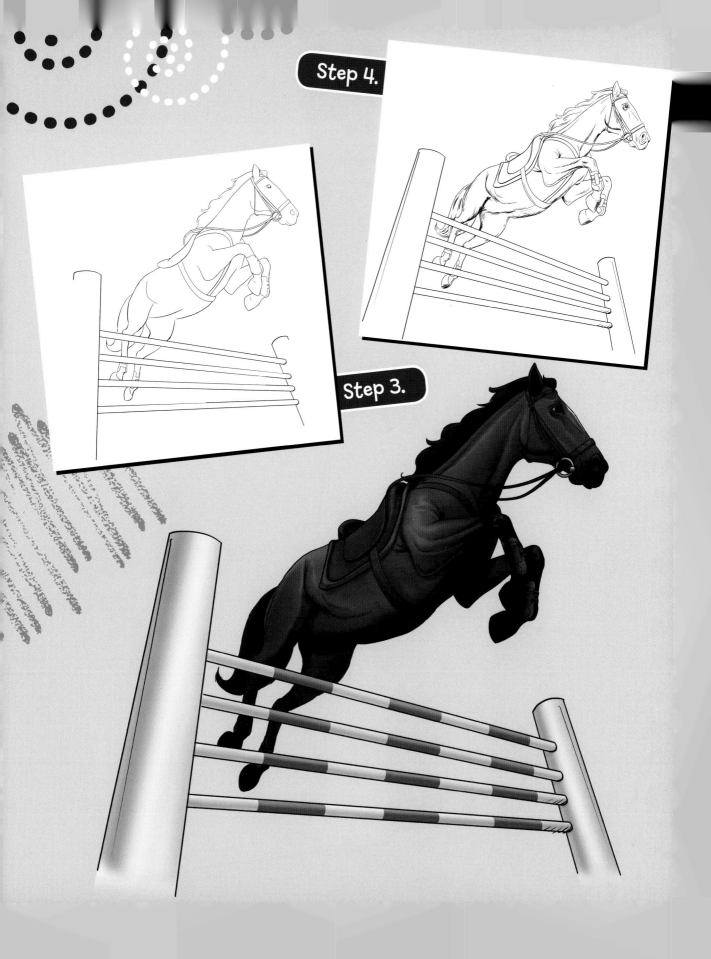

Step 4.

Step 3.

TREAT FACE

Many horses will do anything for food. Favorite treats include apples, peppermints, and carrots. Some horses even learn to drink soda from cans or steal chips from open bags! This appaloosa is up-close and personal, while waiting for his snack.

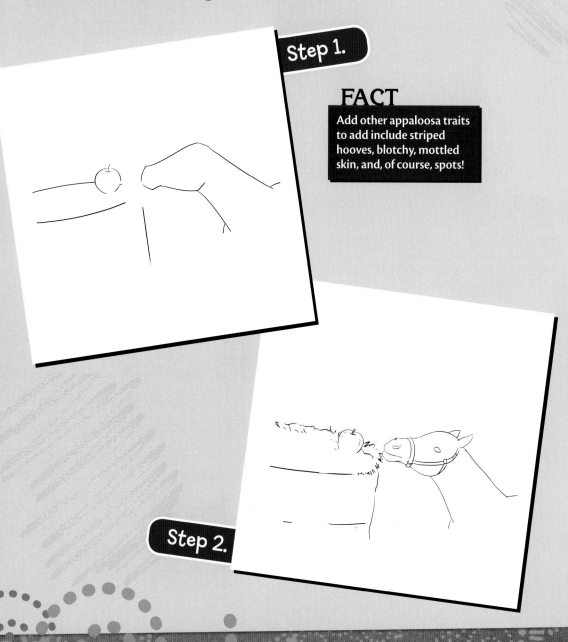

Step 1.

FACT

Add other appaloosa traits to add include striped hooves, blotchy, mottled skin, and, of course, spots!

Step 2.

Step 3.

Step 4.

SPLASHED IN PAINT

American paint horses come in any color mixed with white. Experiment by mixing the shape and size of the horse's spots. It's time to get creative!

Step 1.

Step 2.

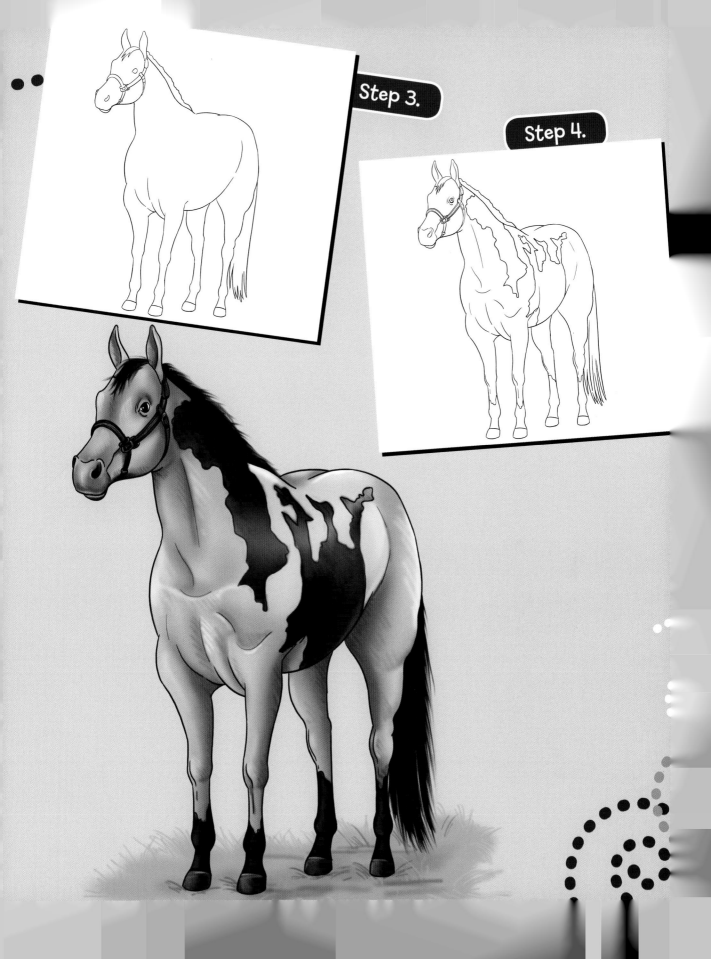

Step 3.

Step 4.

BONDING

Mares show affection for their foals by nuzzling, licking, and sniffing. Like this mother, they are usually protective for the first few weeks of the foal's life. After that, they allow their colts or fillies to do more exploring.

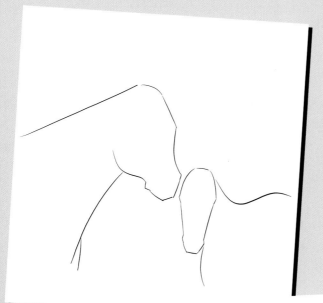

Step 1.

Tip

Draw the rest of this foal's body, including its long legs and short, curly tail.

Step 2.

SPOTTED SCENERY

Spotted horses have been seen around the world. They have been called Celestial Horses, Tigres, and Knabstruppers. In North America, they are appaloosas. Named after the Palouse River in Washington and Idaho, appaloosas have become a symbol of American history.

Step 1.

Tip

The Appaloosa Horse Club holds a Heritage class. Competitors wear costumes that shows off the breed's history. Anything except American Indian costumes may be entered. Draw your appaloosa in authentic trappings and win the class!

Step 2.

Step 3.

Step 4.

INTERNET SITES

FactHound offers a safe, fun way to find Internet sites related to this book. All of the sites on FactHound have been researched by our staff.

Here's all you do:

Visit *www.facthound.com*

Type in this code: 9781476540016

Super-cool stuff!

Check out projects, games and lots more at
www.capstonekids.com

LOOK FOR ALL THE BOOKS IN THIS SERIES

Drawing Appaloosas
and Other Handsome Horses

Drawing Friesians
and Other Beautiful Horses

Drawing Arabians
and Other Amazing Horses

Drawing Mustangs
and Other Wild Horses

Drawing Barrel Racers
and Other Speedy Horses

Drawing Thoroughbreds
and Other Elegant Horses